ROOTS AND REVELATIONS

Navigating Today's Adoption Path

Yellow Dress Ink.

Copyright © 2025. All rights reserved.

No part of this publication may be copied, reproduced in any format, by any means, electronic or otherwise, without prior consent from the copyright owner and publisher of this book

TABLE OF CONTENTS

About the Author	iv
Introduction	vi
Chapter 1: Understanding the Adoption Journey	1
Chapter 2: Infancy & Early Childhood	5
Chapter 3: The School-Age Years	8
Chapter 4 : The Adolescent Years	17
Chapter 5 : Building and Integrating the Child's Story	24
Chapter 6: Fostering Identity Through Culture & Heritage	27
Chapter 7: Navigating Birth Family Connections & Complex Emotions	30
Tips for Using This Journal	39

ABOUT THE AUTHOR

As someone who was adopted as an infant, I've lived through the complexities of adoption firsthand. I was born to my biological mother but raised by my adoptive family. I wrestled early on with questions about my identity and belonging. Growing up, I often wondered who I resembled, both inside and out, and whether there were parts of me that reflected the woman who gave birth to me. Over time, I've discovered that adoption is not the end of a story but rather the beginning of a profound journey marked by love, courage, and, at times, loss.

My childhood was filled with the ordinary joys of family life, holidays, bedtime stories, new friendships, and the quieter moments of wondering about my origins. These internal explorations led me to see how critical it is for parents and children to honor the layers of family history and hold space for a wide range of emotions. Every adopted child deserves to know their story in a way that fosters connection, self-esteem, and a respectful view of the past.

As an adult, I've continued to learn about adoption from multiple perspectives: research, connecting with other adoptees and adoptive parents, and examining my own evolving feelings about my birth and adoptive families. This book culminates my journey toward embracing my identity, reconciling my questions, and finding peace in the duality of being born to one family and raised by another. By sharing insights and practical strategies, I hope to offer adoptive parents a deeper understanding of the inner landscape of an adopted child.

Thank you for allowing me to share my story and experiences with you. Adoption, as I've realized, is a lifelong dance of healing, empathy, and understanding, all powered by the profound capacity of unconditional love.

"A child born to another woman calls me mom. The magnitude of that tragedy and the depth of that privilege are not lost on me." – Jody Landers.

INTRODUCTION

Adoption is not the end of a process; it's the beginning of a beautifully complex story. This book is written for adoptive parents like you who want to nurture their children with understanding, empathy, and unwavering acceptance.

Inside these pages, you'll find insights, strategies, and hands-on activities designed to help you build and sustain deep connections with your child. Whether you are in the early stages of adoption or years into parenting, I aim to offer fresh perspectives and practical tools. Out of deep love and respect, I will refer to my adoptive parents simply as my parents throughout this book.

Every adopted child has a unique story that deserves respect, honesty, and celebration. Just as significantly, I recognize that every adoptive parent needs support in navigating the emotional landscape of adoption, the uncertainties, the unexpected questions, and the sometimes-conflicting feelings that arise.

Consider this guide my way of walking alongside you. It is structured to address essential topics such as building emotional security, understanding your child's background, embracing cultural roots, and fostering a sense of belonging. You'll also find activities to encourage healthy expression and strengthen family bonds.

The last pages give you a chance to reflect. Use it as a journal, to sort out your thoughts. Even if writing isn't your thing, consider the prompts during moments of mediation.

Welcome to a new chapter in your family's story that only you and your child can write together.

CHAPTER 1

Understanding the Adoption Journey

A clear overview of adoption, common challenges, and the emotional landscape for parents and children.

Personal Reflection

When I look at the photos my parents have of me as a baby, taken soon after I arrived in their home, I can't help but notice the anxious expression on my face despite being only a few months old. My dad often joked about how worried I always looked back then. As I got older, I started imagining what that tiny baby must have felt.

I was born on October 22 and almost immediately taken from my biological mother's arms. At the time, mothers who planned to place their children for adoption weren't allowed to keep their babies in their hospital rooms. My birth mother would have stayed on a separate floor, away from the sounds of other new families bonding.

After spending some time in the hospital, I was placed in a foster home on October 31, the chaos of Halloween likely swirling around someone's front door as I arrived in an unfamiliar place. Of course, I looked worried! I had been taken away from the woman who gave birth to me, handed over to a stranger, and dropped into an entirely new world.

Adoption Basics

Adoption sits at the intersection of hope, responsibility, and transformation. It's more than a legal process; it's a lifelong experience that reshapes the lives of both parents and children.

When a family chooses to adopt, they enter a new stage of parenthood, rich with rewards but filled with unique hurdles. Recognizing from the start that adoption brings together different histories, emotions, and cultural backgrounds can help set the foundation for a healthier, more resilient family bond.

Many parents approach adoption with high hopes, eager to open their hearts and homes. But while love is an important starting point, it's also necessary to understand the many ways adoption can influence a child's sense of identity, security, and emotional growth. Being aware of these factors gives families the tools to navigate the challenges that come with bringing a child from a different home or even a different culture into their own.

Different Types of Adoption

One of the first steps in adoption is deciding which path to follow.

1. **Domestic Adoption**: Adopting a child within the same country, often through agencies, lawyers, or private arrangements. This can be an open adoption, where some form of contact with the birth family is maintained, or a closed adoption, depending on everyone's preferences and circumstances.
2. **International Adoption**: Parents bring a child into their home from another country, navigating immigration laws and additional paperwork, and sometimes travel to the child's birth country. This path can introduce cultural and linguistic differences but also offers opportunities to integrate new traditions.
3. **Foster-to-Adopt**: Fostering a child who may eventually become legally free for adoption. This process can be rewarding but may involve uncertainty, as reunification with the birth family is the initial priority.
4. **Kinship Adoption:** A family member or close friend adopts a biologically related child. This approach helps preserve family ties and cultural heritage but requires clear communication, defined roles, and emotional boundaries.

Each type of adoption carries responsibilities and complexities, and selecting the right path depends on a family's resources, comfort level, and long-term vision.

Myths vs. Realities About Adoption

Although adoption is more recognized and accepted than ever, many myths still linger, causing unnecessary worry or unrealistic expectations.

- **Myth:** An adopted child will automatically struggle more than a child raised by biological parents.
- **Reality:** All children face challenges. Some adopted children have extra questions about identity or grief, but with the right support, many thrive just as well as their peers.
- **Myth:** A strong bond can only form if the child is adopted as an infant.
- **Reality:** Attachment develops through consistent care, empathy, and time, no matter when a child joins the family.
- **Myth:** Talking about a child's birth family will undermine the adoptive parents' role.
- **Reality:** Celebrating a child's origins and welcoming their questions can strengthen trust and deepen family bonds.

Letting go of these myths helps families approach adoption with open minds and a willingness to embrace its complexities.

CHAPTER 2

Infancy & Early Childhood

Creating a Safe Emotional Space

Consistent routines such as regular bedtimes and mealtimes help infants and toddlers feel secure, especially if they've experienced early disruptions. Even small changes can cause distress, so responding gently and calmly reassures them.

A predictable environment is especially important for adopted children, as uncertainty can trigger feelings of past transitions or losses. Establishing daily rituals, like a nightly bedtime story or a regular weekend walk, sends a clear message: your home is stable and reliable. This consistency helps children feel safe enough to express their emotions and trust in their surroundings.

Communication plays a key role in emotional security. Active listening means giving your child your full attention, putting away distractions, maintaining eye contact, and reflecting on what they say. A simple phrase like, "I hear that you're disappointed we couldn't visit your friend today," validates their feelings. Using reflective language shows them you are truly listening, helping them develop emotional maturity. Over time, this creates a home environment where feelings can be expressed and explored without fear of judgment.

Introducing the Child's Adoption Story Simply

Use clear, age-appropriate language when explaining adoption. For example: "You grew in your birth mother's belly, but she wanted you to be safe, so she helped you find us." Repeating this narrative regularly, like a bedtime story, helps normalize adoption.

As your child grows, add details gradually, ensuring they feel comfortable discussing their origins. Brief, positive mentions of their birth parents prevent secrecy or shame. This approach fosters an open and honest conversation about adoption, allowing your child to understand their story at their own pace.

Understanding Attachment Styles

Attachment is the bond between a child and their caregiver, shaping how they see themselves, others, and the world. Secure attachment develops when children receive consistent nurturing hugs, kind words, and quick responses to their needs. They feel safe enough to explore, knowing their caregiver is there for them. They also learn that expressing emotions, both positive and negative, is accepted and supported.

If early experiences involve inconsistency, neglect, or trauma, insecure attachment may form instead:

- Anxious attachment: The child clings to their caregiver, fearing abandonment.
- Avoidant attachment: The child pulls away, preferring to handle emotions alone.
- Disorganized attachment: The child shifts unpredictably between seeking closeness and rejecting it.
- Adopted children may struggle with secure attachment due to early disruptions in care. Recognizing these patterns helps parents respond with empathy instead of unintentionally reinforcing fears.

The good news is that attachment can be strengthened. Tangible steps include:

- Keeping predictable routines (consistent meals, bedtimes, and one-on-one time).
- Offering affectionate touch (hugs, back rubs, or playful interactions).
- Engaging in meaningful conversations (asking about their day and showing genuine interest).

These steady, loving interactions build trust, helping your child feel valued and secure in their relationships.

CHAPTER 3

The School-Age Years

Balancing Reality and Reassurance

Personal Reflection

The baby book my mother made for me was meticulously put together. She recorded practically every day of my life for the first few years and then every week after that how tall I was, what I ate, even the locks of my hair. It was beautifully done. Right at the front of the book was a family tree filled with my adoptive family's history.

Since my adoption was closed, my parents only had limited, non-identifying information, which wasn't included.

I did know my extended adoptive family and spent summers with my grandparents and cousins, making some of my best memories. I'm grateful for the tree as it is, but at the same time, it doesn't feel like it truly reflects my complete set of roots.

School-age children might ask, "Why couldn't my birth parents keep me?" Offer honest, gentle answers: "They loved you but couldn't be the parents you needed at the time." These moments can become opportunities. By talking openly about your family's story, you give your child the tools and confidence to respond: "I'm adopted, and this is my awesome family." Acknowledge their sadness while reinforcing that they are loved and wanted.

Children begin to engage more with the outside world during these years (roughly ages 5–12). Assignments like family tree projects can be challenging if they don't fit the usual model. Peers may ask blunt questions. These moments are opportunities to celebrate your child's adoption story and help them respond with confidence.

Encourage identity exploration by reading adoption-themed books, discussing birth family traits, or talking about the day they joined your home. Consistent reassurance that they are loved and chosen instills pride in their background.

You can also promote confidence by normalizing adoption in everyday conversation. If a teacher assigns a family tree, brainstorm ways to include both birth and adoptive relatives. Let your child decide what feels right for them.

Why Love Alone Isn't Enough: Understanding Your Child's Unique Emotional Needs

Personal Reflection

When I was little, people often said, 'You look so much like your mother,' and I'd smile, thinking it must be true if everyone said it. But as soon as I started to understand what it meant to be adopted, that I shared no biology with my mother, those words began to sting. Even so, whenever I heard them, I'd glance at her face and see how happy she looked. Instead of feeling proud or comforted, I felt uneasy, like we were both pretending.

What made it worse was watching my (adoptive) sister. She looked so much like our father and his sisters. She also played the piano with remarkable skill, like my grandmother and aunts on my dad's side. I tried, but I could never match their level of talent. No one ever told me I'd inherited a gift from my dad's side, and I couldn't help wondering which parts of me came from my birth family.

Over time, hearing 'You look so much like your mother' stopped feeling like a compliment and started feeling like a lie. Each time I saw my mother's pleased smile it only deepened my sense of betrayal. Instead of bringing us closer, those words drove me further into the uneasy reality that I may never know who I looked like.

Affection alone doesn't automatically guarantee a child's emotional security. Many adopted children carry their histories with them. Some may have moved between multiple caregivers, while others feel a deep sense of loss tied to their birth family. Some may wonder why they were adopted or if they truly belong. Attentive parents recognize that these concerns require more than love. They require patience, empathy, and a commitment to listening without judgment.

Creating a safe emotional space means encouraging questions

and conversations instead of brushing them aside. It means being open to discussing a child's birth story and respecting their curiosity about their origins. Over time, consistent routines, celebrating their heritage, and gently exploring their personal story can help them feel more secure.

Love might begin the adoption journey, but a deeper understanding of a child's history, emotions, and developmental needs is what strengthens the relationship and fosters true belonging.

The Child's Perspective: Potential Feelings of Loss, Confusion, or Loyalty Conflicts

Personal Reflection

My father died in his mid-eighties after a very brief illness. During one of our last private conversations, he asked if I'd ever found my birth mother. To say I was shocked is an understatement. Why now? I wondered. After all these years? Did he not realize how opening that dialogue sooner could have brought us so much closer and maybe even changed the course of my life?

'Yes,' I told him. He said, 'I always wondered if you did. Don't ever tell your mother.' At that moment, I realized he honestly didn't grasp how much acknowledging my history mattered. I wanted to tell him how hard it had been for me, the shame I felt, and the inner turmoil of keeping secrets to protect my parents from my truth. I wanted to explain the sadness I carried when my birth mother died far too young and the guilt over not letting her be part of my life or meet her grandchildren. But I said nothing.

From a child's perspective, adoption can stir up a mix of excitement and uncertainty. While there's often relief and gratitude in joining a loving home, there can also be an undercurrent of loss.

Children, no matter how young, may grieve the family or life they left behind, even if they don't fully remember it. This can show up as sadness, anger, or an overwhelming need for reassurance. Some feel confused trying to juggle two families, wondering why their birth parents couldn't raise them, or worrying about having more than one set of parents.

These emotions can lead to loyalty conflicts, with a child torn between loving both families. They might hold back on asking about their birth family for fear of upsetting their adoptive parents or worry that loving their adoptive family somehow betrays their birth parents. This internal struggle can make them test boundaries or withdraw as they try to figure out where they belong.

By acknowledging these complicated emotions, adoptive parents can create a supportive space where a child can piece together their story without feeling pressured to choose sides.

Interactive Focus: "Question Jar"

Purpose:

- To give the child a safe, ongoing way to ask questions about adoption (or anything else).
- To foster trust and openness in family communication.

How to Do It:

1. Decorate a jar or box together and label it with something like "Ask Me Anything" or "Question Jar."
2. Encourage the child to write down (or dictate, if younger) questions anytime they arise. These could be about adoption, birth family, or deeper feelings.
3. Set a regular time each week (e.g., "Question Jar Wednesday") to read and discuss the questions as a family.
4. Reinforce that no question is off-limits or "wrong."
5. If a question is challenging, it's okay to say, "I need some time to think about how to answer this best. Let's come back to it." The key is following up.

Adoptive Parent Emotions: Mixed Feelings: Joy, Anxiety, Impostor Syndrome, or Fear of Not Measuring Up

For adoptive parents, holding their child for the first time can spark a swirl of emotions, from overwhelming joy to deep anxiety. On one hand, there's the excitement of finally being called "Mom" or "Dad." On the other, doubts and fears may creep in.

A common struggle is impostor syndrome, a persistent worry that they are somehow less legitimate or less capable than their biological parents. This inner voice may whisper fears that they are unworthy or that their child deserves someone "better."

Adding to these concerns is the weight of societal expectations. Adoptive parents might feel the need to prove themselves to show friends and family that their child is thriving and that they are capable. They may also wonder whether navigating birth family questions or addressing their child's potential trauma will overshadow the simple joys of parenting.

Balancing the joy of finally having a child to love with the anxiety of meeting their emotional, mental, and physical needs can feel overwhelming. Recognizing these mixed feelings is the first step in normalizing them. It helps parents accept that it's entirely possible to feel profoundly grateful and deeply uncertain at the same time.

Tips for Self-Care and Seeking Support (Therapy, Support Groups, Online Communities)

Reflection for Parents

It's easy to focus so much on your child's emotions that you neglect your own. But taking a step back to understand your reactions can help you be a calmer, more supportive parent. Here are a few ways to stay in touch with yourself:

Journaling Prompts

- **Emotional Triggers:** What moments leave you feeling stressed or impatient? Write down how you felt and why.
- **Coping with Stress:** What methods have you tried (walking, talking to a friend, deep breathing)? Which ones helped? What would you like to try?

- **Handling Your Child's Big Feelings:** Think of a time your child had a major meltdown. How did you respond? What might you do differently next time?

Importance of Ongoing Self-Awareness in Parenting

Parenting is always evolving, and so are you. Paying attention to your emotions, habits, and thought patterns helps you respond to your child with more empathy. By staying curious about your own growth, you show your child that learning and adapting are normal parts of life.

Caring for a child, especially one who has experienced loss, trauma, or multiple transitions, requires emotional resilience. This is why self-care isn't a luxury—it's a necessity. Simple practices like journaling, meditation, or setting aside downtime can make a difference. Many parents find comfort in leaning on their partner, extended family, or close friends for practical help and emotional support.

Beyond personal networks, professional guidance can be invaluable. Adoption-informed therapists understand the complexities of attachment and can offer coping strategies tailored to your situation.

If adoption followed experiences of infertility, failed IVF cycles, miscarriages, or even the loss of a child, those past griefs may resurface. The adoption process itself can magnify that pain, serving as a reminder of a biological connection or dream that wasn't fully realized. It's normal to feel sadness or longing during this transition. Rather than pushing these feelings aside, allow yourself space to mourn. Processing grief can help you move forward with a more open heart for your adopted child.

Equally important is connecting with others who share similar experiences. In-person and online support groups provide a safe space to discuss challenges, celebrate progress, and connect with people who truly understand.

By seeking support and acknowledging the emotional layers of adoption, you'll feel less isolated and gain new perspectives for navigating the ups and downs of parenting.

CHAPTER 4

The Adolescent Years

Personal Reflection

By the time I turned sixteen, my need to learn the details of my adoption became an obsession. At home, the subject was off-limits. I never understood why, but I assumed it must be shameful. Maybe my mother felt judged for not having another biological child. Could she have? Why did they choose to adopt me? I felt indebted to them in a strange way. The story I heard growing up was that they 'rescued' me, but from what, I had no idea. All I knew was that I owed them somehow.

When I finally met my birth mother, Paula, and her family, it was complicated. After waiting 25 years to meet the woman who brought me into the world, it was hard to say I wanted to keep things at arm's length. Trying to juggle all those emotions was overwhelming.

Adolescence

The teen years bring identity to the forefront, especially for adoptees. Curiosity about biological roots may intensify. Questions about shared traits or health history can arise. Rebellion can also surface, often as a way for teens to assert independence and figure out where they belong.

Keeping communication open is key. Sharing age-appropriate information, listening to their frustrations, and allowing them to participate in decisions such as seeking contact with birth relatives builds trust. Your ongoing support, even when they push you away, reassures them they're not alone in exploring their identity.

Heightened Identity Exploration

Adolescence is a time when identity takes center stage, especially for adoptees. It's common for teens to wonder more about their birth family, their origins, and how they fit into the bigger picture. This curiosity often fuels a need for answers: What do my birth parents look like? Do we share the same talents, health history, or personality traits? These are not just passing thoughts; they play a key role in self-discovery.

During this period, some teens may also rebel, pushing boundaries, questioning rules, or even challenging their adoptive family's authority. While this can be frustrating, it's often a sign of their need for autonomy and a way to establish their own identity.

Keeping the conversation open helps. Even when their questions are complex or sensitive, letting them know you're there to listen without judgment matters. If they want to learn more about their birth family, providing honest (but age-appropriate) information builds trust and shows respect for their feelings.

Consistent support is what matters most. Whether that means being a listening ear, sharing what you know, or helping them find resources like support groups or counseling, your willingness to stand by them makes a difference.

A teen may want to contact birth relatives or look them up online. It's normal for adoptive parents to feel anxiety or fear of rejection. Staying calm and offering guidance reassures them that they're supported no matter what they discover.

Personal Reflection

When I was in high school, I went through a major rebellious phase. My mom and I were constantly at each other's throats, and I absolutely hated all the rules. Honestly, I felt like I didn't fit in anywhere, which led to what I now jokingly call 'over-friending.' I was so desperate for connection that I'd call people nonstop, show up uninvited, and give over-the-top gifts that made everyone uncomfortable. Of course, they'd eventually push me away, and I'd end up feeling even more lonely.

At the same time, I became extremely empathetic, almost to a fault. I finally connected with the right therapist, who told me this was common among adoptees. Subconsciously, I felt like I had been rescued, so I thought everyone else should be too.

I realize now how much of this was tied to my shaky sense of identity and confidence. I'm still very empathetic. It's both a blessing and a challenge.

Interactive Focus: "Me & You" Journal

Sometimes, it's easier to write things down than to talk them out face-to-face. The Me & You Journal gives your child a private, low-pressure way to share thoughts at their own pace.

How-To:

- Label a Notebook: Choose a simple notebook and decorate it together.
- Encourage Back-and-Forth Notes: Keep it in an easily accessible spot. If your child wants to share a question, thought, or feeling, they can write or draw it inside. You respond in writing, creating a safe cycle of communication.

Over time, this shared journal becomes a record of your private talks, something you can both look back on for comfort. It also gives you time to think about your responses instead of feeling pressured to reply on the spot. This simple book can build trust, strengthen your connection, and show your child that their voice matters.

Empathy as a Tool: Responding Calmly to Big Emotions

When children, especially those with adoption-related trauma or unresolved losses, experience intense emotions, they need guidance to navigate them. Empathy is your greatest ally in this process. Instead of immediately trying to fix a problem or dismiss their feelings, take a breath and acknowledge the child's emotions first. Being empathetic means being present with your child in their struggle, not solving it for them.

Responding calmly is essential. If you mirror your child's intensity with frustration or anger, it can amplify their distress. Instead, maintain a gentle tone and a relaxed posture. Sometimes, offering physical reassurance, like a comforting pat on the back or a warm hug, can ease tension. By pairing empathy with consistency and active listening, you create an atmosphere where a child feels heard, safe, and supported, even during overwhelming moments.

The Importance of Validating These Emotions Early On

Early validation of a child's emotions lays the foundation for open communication and trust. When children sense that their parents are willing to hear their worries or grief, they begin to internalize the message that their feelings are valid and worthy of attention. Simple yet intentional responses, such as, "It's okay to miss your birth family" or "I understand that you might feel sad or confused," can offer profound relief.

Validation isn't about fixing every painful feeling or providing all the answers immediately. Instead, it means being fully present, listening attentively, and reassuring the child that their emotions are acceptable.

Over time, this approach can reduce anxiety, strengthen the parent-child bond, and foster a deeper sense of security as the child grows.

Interactive Focus: Weekly Connection Ritual

Setting aside time each week for a simple, enjoyable routine strengthens trust and emotional closeness. A "connection ritual" allows the whole family to pause their busy routines and focus on one another.

Examples

- Gratitude Circle: Pick a comfortable spot, like the living room or kitchen table, and let each person share something they're thankful for that week.
- Feelings Check-In: Take five or ten minutes for each family member to name a feeling they've experienced that day or week: happy, sad, nervous, excited, or anything else.

Planning a Regular Family Ritual That Feels Natural and Fun

- Choose a Specific Day/Time: For example, Sunday night

after dinner or Saturday morning before the day begins.
- Keep It Short: 10 to 15 minutes is often enough. Consistency matters more than length.
- Let the Kids Help: Ask for their input. Involving them increases their sense of ownership.
- Be Flexible: If someone is tired or cranky, simplify. If a new idea works better, try it. The ritual can evolve as your family's needs change.

CHAPTER 5

Building and Integrating the Child's Story

Why Narrative Matters

Stories aren't just for bedtime; they help us understand who we are. For an adopted child, making sense of their past and how it connects to their present can be essential for feeling whole.

When you talk openly about the time before they joined your family, you show them that their story didn't begin the day they came home. Acknowledging their earlier experiences can strengthen their self-esteem by reinforcing that every part of their journey matters.

The Child's Sense of Identity from Birth to Present

As mentioned in an earlier chapter, adopted children often wonder, "Where did I come from? Who do I look like?" Providing honest, age-appropriate answers helps them feel more secure.

For younger children, a simple explanation might be enough: "Your birth mom wanted you to be safe, so she made sure you found us." As they grow older, they may ask deeper questions about why their birth parents made certain choices or what their early days were like. Giving the right amount of detail at each stage helps them understand how their past shapes who they are today.

Being honest doesn't mean revealing everything at once, especially when parts of their story are complex. Share their history in small pieces, checking in to see how they process the information. Over time, this approach builds trust because they learn they can rely on you for real answers.

Some parts of a child's past may be difficult to discuss. Including both the positive and painful moments shows them that their entire story is valid. It also helps them see that their life is made up of many threads, birth, and adoption, that weave together into a unique narrative.

Interactive Focus: Timeline of "Becoming Us"

Purpose:

- Visually illustrate the child's life timeline, including their birth and the day they joined the adoptive family.
- Create a safe space for children to ask questions about significant events in their history.

Materials Needed:

- Long roll of paper or poster board
- Markers, photos, stickers

How to Do It:

1. Draw a horizontal line and mark the child's birth date at one end.
2. Identify key life events (first steps, birthdays, moves, meeting new siblings).
3. Mark the date the child joined the family and continue adding milestones up to the present.
4. Invite the child to write or draw their thoughts about events they find meaningful.

CHAPTER 6

Fostering Identity Through Culture & Heritage

Celebrate the Child's Birth Culture and Integrate It into Everyday Life

Cultural Identity and Self-Esteem

Adolescents may seek deeper ways to explore their birth culture, such as learning the language, joining cultural groups, or even visiting their birth country. They may also struggle with feeling caught between two cultures. Support and empathy can help them navigate this identity balance.

Why Maintaining Ties to Heritage Supports Belonging

Feeling connected to their birth culture can boost an adopted child's confidence. Our backgrounds, traditions, and family histories shape how we see ourselves. For an adopted child, learning about their birth culture sends a clear message: Your story matters! This connection can help them feel more grounded, and proud of who they are.

How to Learn About and Honor the Child's Birth Culture

- Start Small: Introduce children's books, traditional music, or art projects from their birth culture.
- Celebrate Holidays and Festivals: Attend local cultural events or recreate traditions at home.
- Learn the Language (Even Just a Little): Simple words and phrases show genuine investment in their heritage.
- Seek Out Cultural Communities: Workshops, dance lessons, or social gatherings can connect your child to others with the same heritage.

Interactive Focus: "Where I'm from" Poem or Booklet

Poem Approach

- Brainstorm foods, holiday traditions, favorite songs, or special words from both your family's culture and your child's birth culture.
- Weave them into a simple poem: "I am from [favorite food], from [holiday tradition] ..."

Booklet Option

- Turn each line of the poem into its own page.
- Let your child illustrate or add photos.
- This mini-book becomes a keepsake that honors both your heritage and theirs.

Reflection for Parents: Exploring Heritage and Introducing New Traditions

Make Everyone Feel Seen

- Ask for input from all family members.
- Stay curious; your enthusiasm shows your child that their culture is worth celebrating.
- Create an inclusive environment in which these traditions become part of the entire family's story.

Keep It Conversational

- Ask your child how they feel about each new tradition.
- Allow them to have mixed feelings.
- Show that you're open to adapting or trying different approaches as you learn together.

CHAPTER 7

Navigating Birth Family Connections & Complex Emotions

Purpose: Supporting a Child's Curiosity, Grief, and Questions About Their Birth Family

Every adopted child processes their birth family connection differently. Your role as a parent is to create a safe space for these emotions, whether curiosity, grief, or confusion, to unfold. There is no right or wrong way for a child to explore their birth roots. What matters is that they feel comfortable talking to you openly and without hesitation.

Acknowledging Loss and Grief

Adoption is a meaningful way to build a family, but it also begins with loss. Even the most loving adoptive homes can't erase the separation from a birth parent. Let your child know that it's normal to grieve. Reassure them: It's okay to be sad or miss your birth family.

Grief may show up differently depending on your child's age.

- Young children might ask simple questions like, "Do they miss me?"
- Older children and teens may express anger or confusion.

Validate all of these feelings.

Personal Reflection

While sorting through my parents' house after my father passed away, I discovered little reminders of my adoption and early childhood. One was a Polaroid of me in a lemon-yellow dress. It wasn't dated, but I was very young. In the same box was a small white paper bag, and inside it was that exact dress. I took it out and, without really thinking, held it up to my nose. Maybe it was just a reflex. There was also a tiny silver heart with a handwritten note that read, 'Pinned on the baby when she first arrived.' A few more keepsakes were in there, some with my name spelled wrong. Why didn't my parents ever share these things with me? That little dress held so much love that it belonged to me.

Interactive Focus: "Letter to My Birth Family"

A Safe Outlet for Thoughts and Questions

Writing an unsent letter can help a child or teen process gratitude, curiosity, anger, sorrow, or any mix of emotions without pressure. If contact is possible, they can decide later whether to send it. If not, the act of writing can still be healing.

Deciding Whether to Send the Letter

- If the adoption is open or semi-open, discuss what your child hopes will happen if they send it.
- If the adoption is closed, acknowledge the loss of direct contact and reassure your child that their feelings still matter.

Parents' Role

- Listen without judgment.
- Let your child decide whether to share, keep private, or eventually send the letter.
- Reassure them that loving or missing their birth family doesn't diminish their bond with you.

Balancing Expectations and Reality

Many adoptees believe that meeting their birth family will magically fill in all the missing pieces. The truth? It's rarely that simple.

Personal Reflection

When I finally met Paula, my birth mother, I was pregnant with my first son. I was focused on getting my medical history, but I was also deeply curious about her decision to put me up for adoption. How could she carry me for nine months and then let me go?

Would I ever really understand her reasons if I couldn't bring myself to ask? Those thoughts stayed with me for a long time. I learned the hard way that even when you make contact, you might not get the closure you imagined.

It was complicated. I saw no benefit in telling my adoptive parents, so I kept the reunion to myself. Over time, I had come to respect that my adoptive family viewed me as their daughter, and the circumstances of my birth weren't something they ever wanted to discuss. Even so, finally meeting the woman I had waited 25 years to see was difficult enough; telling her I needed to keep our relationship at arm's length felt even harder.

It's a delicate balance for which anyone in this situation needs to prepare. We often imagine that meeting our birth family will fill in every missing piece, but it's rarely so straightforward or comforting.

If I had known the full story of my birth or felt comfortable enough to ask, maybe the reunion wouldn't have been so stressful or even necessary.

Paula's family was large, welcoming, and excited to meet me. Sitting around their table that first time, it felt oddly familiar, like I belonged. They gave me a photo album, and the first picture was of Paula and my birth father. She and I were very much alike our styles, our laughs. She was bold but kind, the kind of person who lit up a room. Though Paula and I kept in touch, she honored my request to keep our visits limited. Over time, I learned she had battled depression and anxiety other similarities we shared. She also struggled with addiction. She eventually went to rehab and stayed sober for years. She sent me the occasional card or painting she made. We talked on the phone. She tried reaching out to Mike now and then. I spoke to him once. We promised to keep in touch but never did.

I told Paula that because she was much younger than my adoptive parents, we still had time for her to truly know me and to meet my now 17- and 20-year-old sons. I didn't want my kids to feel burdened by secrets or forced to choose between families, so they knew everything from the start.

Paula married after I was born and had two more children. My half-siblings, raised by their father in another province, didn't see Paula much either. One day, I received an email out of the blue from Tina, my half-sister, asking me to call her.

Paula had been found dead. She was discovered in her apartment, alone with her dog. A "natural" death. It shattered me. None of those imagined trips, the laughter, the conversations would ever happen. She would never meet her grandchildren, and I would never hear the rest of her story.

I knew she had thought about me on my birthday, on Mother's Day, and on many other days. I told her I appreciated her decision to let me be adopted. I had a good life.

The guilt and sadness were overwhelming. I can't begin to fathom how Paula felt permitted to open the door to my life but never truly walked through it. I went to her funeral with my oldest son, and my extended family tried hard to make us feel included. It stung deeply to learn my name wasn't mentioned in her obituary.

I never asked why. Not everyone knew I existed. Or I wanted to believe I was truly part of a family.

It's been almost ten years since she died. I still have some contact with her family. They live far away, and we don't speak often.

Then, with the popularity of DNA testing, more uncertainty arrived. Mike was not my birth father. Suddenly, I had a whole new set of family members, some uninterested in figuring out our connection and a few who were. Unfortunately, my birth father had recently passed away. Whether he knew I existed remains a mystery, as does whether Paula knew his true identity.

I contacted Paula's family, pressing for answers. It turned out there was much I had never been told. The uncertainty of my birth father's identity and the revelation that Paula had likely died by suicide was the most profound.

An innate distrust takes hold when you long for answers and think you've found them, only to realize the truth remains elusive. All these years later, everything circles back to that very beginning: unanswered questions, missing pieces, and relationships lost to time and circumstance. Yet, even with so much still unknown, I've learned that family by blood or by bond is rarely straightforward. Sometimes, it's full of warmth. Other times, it's heartbreak. But it's ours to navigate and make sense of however we can.

When Professional Help Is Needed

Signs a Child May Benefit from an Adoption-Specialized Therapist

- Persistent sadness, anxiety, or anger
- Withdrawal or trouble forming relationships
- Extreme reactions to adoption topics
- Low self-esteem or negative self-talk
- Feeling "stuck" on questions about birth family that cause ongoing distress

Seeking therapy doesn't mean something is "wrong" with your child. It can be a proactive step to help them navigate complex emotions, especially if they've experienced trauma or multiple placements.

Reflection for Parents

Exploring Your Own Emotions Around the Birth Family

It's normal to feel protective, uncertain, or even insecure when your child shows interest in their birth family. Permit yourself to explore these feelings through journaling, talking to other adoptive parents, or seeking professional guidance.

Balancing Protective Instincts with a Child's Need for Information

Ask yourself: "Am I withholding information because it's best for my child or uncomfortable for me?"

Children need honesty to build trust. Even when details are painful, sharing them gently can deepen your relationship and help your child feel secure.

Personal Reflections

After Tina cleaned out Paula's apartment, a considerable undertaking I should have helped with, she gave me a few mementos: bright red lipstick, beads for a bracelet, and a gold snake ring that wraps around your knuckle.

I pull them out occasionally and laugh.

I also have a small velvet bag containing some of Paula's ashes. I keep thinking about the best way to spread them, but I'm not ready to let her go.

Thank you for taking the time to join me. I've shared pieces of my story, some joyful, some difficult, hoping they shed light on the beauty and complexity of adoption. Over the years, I've realized that the real journey isn't just about finding answers but about discovering myself within many families' deep and tangled roots. By embracing every part of my heritage and experiences, I've found healing, understanding, and a sense of belonging I never thought possible.

I wish you love and happiness as you walk your path, whether you're just beginning to explore adoption, already parenting an adopted child, or supporting someone who is. May this book's insights, reflections, and activities help you build deeper connections, empathy, and peace. Above all, remember that you are not alone. Many have traveled this road before and are cheering you on every step of the way.

I decided to add some prompts for journal writing in continuing the spirit of the "Yellow Dress". You can use these questions as daily or weekly reflections or pick and choose the ones that resonate most with you at any given time. Feel free to write as little or as much as you need—this journal is meant to capture the honest, evolving nature of your adoption journey.

TIPS FOR USING THIS JOURNAL

1. Be Consistent: Aim to spend a few moments each day or week reflecting on a new prompt or revisiting a previous one if you have fresh insights.
2. Stay Honest: This journal is a safe place for you to be completely candid. You don't have to share it with anyone unless you choose to.
3. Allow Room for Evolution: Your answers may change over time—and that's a good thing. Adoption is a journey, and growth is part of it.
4. Optional Sharing: If you're comfortable, consider discussing some reflections with your partner, close family, or a counselor. Sharing can foster understanding and deeper connection.

As you continue your "Yellow Dress" journey, remember that the symbolism of discovering the yellow dress, hidden away yet full of meaning. Revealing the layers of discovery and transformation you'll experience on the adoption path. May these prompts support your healing, growth, and celebration of every milestone along the way.

THE YELLOW DRESS JOURNAL FOR ADOPTIVE PARENTS

1. Reflecting on Expectations

Prompt: Before you began this journey, what did you imagine adoption would be like? How have these expectations shifted as you've progressed through the

Process?

_____

_____

_____

_____

_____

_____

_____

_____

_____

_____

_____

2. Your "Why" for Adoption

Prompt: What made you decide to adopt in the first place? Consider the personal, emotional, or practical reasons that led you here.

_____

_____

_____

_____

_____

_____

_____

_____

_____

_____

_____

_____

_____

_____

3. Worries and Concerns

Prompt: What were your greatest worries before starting the adoption process? Are you still concerned about the same issues, or have new concerns emerged?

_____

_____

_____

_____

_____

_____

_____

_____

_____

_____

_____

_____

_____

_____

4. Reactions from Loved Ones

Prompt: How did your family and friends react when you told them about your plan to adopt? Did their reactions surprise you? How have their feelings evolved?

_____

_____

_____

_____

_____

_____

_____

_____

_____

_____

_____

_____

_____

_____

5. Processing Past Loss

Prompt: Reflect on whether you or your partner experienced any significant loss or hardship prior to choosing adoption. How has that shaped your perspective on Parenting?

_____
_____
_____
_____
_____
_____
_____
_____
_____
_____
_____
_____
_____

6. Considering Other Options

Prompt: Was adoption a first choice, or did you explore other paths to parenthood (e.g., fertility treatments, surrogacy) before deciding to adopt?

Describe how you arrived at this decision.

7. Partnership & Support

Prompt: How would you describe the way your partner is handling the adoption process? Do you feel you're on the same page?

_____

_____

_____

_____

_____

_____

_____

_____

_____

_____

_____

_____

_____

8. Balancing Emotions and Roles

Prompt: Who seems to be coping with the changes better, and why do you think that is? Are there ways you can support each other more effectively?

_____

_____

_____

_____

_____

_____

_____

_____

_____

_____

_____

_____

_____

9. Easing the Process

Prompt: What practical steps or emotional strategies can you implement to make the adoption journey smoother—for yourself, your partner, and your extended circle.

_____

_____

_____

_____

_____

_____

_____

_____

_____

_____

_____

_____

_____

_____

10. Building a Bond

Prompt: Do you feel a natural bond forming with your child? If not, what steps might you take to nurture a deeper connection?

11. Child's Adaptation

Prompt: How do you think your adopted child is adjusting to their new home and family environment? What signs of comfort or stress are you noticing?

_____

_____

_____

_____

_____

_____

_____

_____

_____

_____

_____

12. Birth Family Knowledge

Prompt: What information do you currently have about your child's birth family? How does that information influence your perspective as you parent?

_____
_____
_____
_____
_____
_____
_____
_____
_____
_____
_____
_____
_____
_____

13. Preparing for Questions

Prompt: How ready do you feel to answer your child's questions about their birth family? Are there areas where you'd like to learn or practice more?

_____

_____

_____

_____

_____

_____

_____

_____

_____

_____

_____

_____

_____

14. Your Strengths

Prompt: Name a few personal strengths or qualities you believe will help you address your child's curiosity about their birth family and adoption story.

15. Talking About Birth Families

Prompt: How might your approach differ when your child is very young versus when they become a teenager or adult? Consider how your explanations could evolve over time.

16. Embracing Future Searches

Prompt: In the case of a closed adoption, how do you think you will feel if your child expresses a desire to find their birth family later on? Imagine the emotional response and how you might prepare.

_____

_____

_____

_____

_____

_____

_____

_____

_____

_____

_____

_____

_____

_____

17. Personal Growth

Prompt: What have you learned about yourself during this adoption journey? About your partner? Has this process changed your outlook on parenting or relationships?

_____

_____

_____

_____

_____

_____

_____

_____

_____

_____

_____

_____

_____

18. Daily Gratitude & Reflection

Prompt: Think of something that happened today that filled you with gratitude. Write down what it was and how it made you feel. Then, note one thing you wish you would have handled differently and explore why.

Made in United States
Cleveland, OH
18 December 2025

29032083R00036